# The Owl in the Mirror

Written by Zoë Clarke

Illustrated by Rose Wilkinson

Collins

Grandad always said, "There's looking and there's *looking.*" The first time I climbed up to the attic, all I noticed was broken chairs and boxes of old letters.

But when I *really* looked, there it was, leaning against the brick wall at the back.
A huge old mirror.

The mirror had a large, carved wooden frame. I ran my thumb over the beautiful design.

Birds and animals wrapped themselves around the glass. Hawks and eagles danced at each corner; deer, wrens and wagtails wrestled for space around the edges.

Grandad always said the forest by the house used to be full of birdsong, but it wasn't like that now. I knew there were far fewer birds here now.

Then, at the edge of my vision, I saw something move. When I *really* looked, in the middle of the old mirror, a forest appeared. And in the forest was an owl.

The owl danced along the limb of the tree. It was alive!
When I reached out in the direction of the owl,
the glass felt like ice and my hand disappeared.

I took a deep breath, closed my eyes, and pushed into the icy mirror.

I found myself in a forest, but it wasn't the forest I knew. Everywhere I looked there were living things, dancing in celebration.

Trees with knotted trunks swayed lazily in the wind. I saw something staring down at me from a branch – the owl from the mirror.

Grandad said you could always trust an owl. When it flew to the next tree and looked back at me, I felt it was giving me an instruction to follow, so I did.

As I walked, the forest changed and became less picturesque. The air became heavy, hot and prickly.

Suddenly, there was a smell of burning. The heat from the sun had scorched a dry branch and set it alight.

My vision became blurred, but I could see the birds and animals fleeing from the flames.

The smoke cleared. I could see, at the edge of the forest, a large knotted tree.

The birds and animals moved as one,
leaping and flying into the tree.
The fire burned bright, but
the knotted tree survived.

After the fire had burned out, I saw Grandad chopping the knotted tree down and using the wood to make the frame for the old mirror. As he did so, birds and animals appeared as if they were carved.

The real birds and animals were trapped in the old frame! I knew what I had to do. Measuring my steps back in the direction of the mirror, I pushed into the glass.

Once I was back in the attic, I found Grandad's walking stick. The wooden frame cracked as the stick hit the glass. Birds and animals celebrated as they were freed from their wooden sleep.

The forest was alive again! I saw it all because I was *really* looking. Just like Grandad always said.

# The forest – past and present

# After reading

**Letters and Sounds:** Phases 5–6

**Word count:** 497

**Focus phonemes:** /n/ kn, gn /m/ mb /r/ wr /s/ c, ce /c/ que /zh/ s, si /sh/ ti

**Common exception words:** of, to, the, into, said, do, were, one, once, their, because, beautiful, move, eyes

**Curriculum links:** Art and design; Science: Animals including humans

**National Curriculum learning objectives:** Reading/word reading: apply phonic knowledge and skills as the route to decode words, read common exception words, noting unusual correspondences between spelling and sound and where these occur in the word; read other words of more than one syllable that contain taught GPCs; Reading/comprehension: develop pleasure in reading, motivation to read, vocabulary and understanding by being encouraged to link what they read or hear to their own experiences

## Developing fluency

- Your child may enjoy hearing you read the book.
- Take turns to read a page of the main text, demonstrating how pausing at commas and emphasising words in italics adds drama.

## Phonic practice

- Challenge your child to read these words, identifying the /s/, /sh/ or /zh/ sounds in each. Which word contains a /s/ and /sh/ sound? (*celebration*)

  vision icy celebration noticed direction

- Challenge your child to think of other words where /s/ is spelled with a "c". They could think of words that rhyme with nice and lace. (e.g. *dice*, *lice*, *mice*; *face*, *pace*, *race*)

## Extending vocabulary

- Challenge your child to explain the meaning of these words in the context of the story, and another meaning the word has:
  - page 2: letters (e.g. *correspondence*; *a, b, c*)
  - page 5: wrestled (e.g. *struggled*; *fought in a ring, like wrestlers*)
  - page 7: vision (e.g. *what you see*; *a magical sight*)
  - page 8: limb (e.g. *branch*; *leg or arm*)